Superette

By the same author:

Girlery

Superette

Melinda Bufton

PUNCHER & WATTMANN

First published in 2018
Published by Puncher and Wattmann
PO Box 441
Glebe NSW 2037

http://www.puncherandwattmann.com

puncherandwattmann@bigpond.com

National Library of Australia
Cataloguing-in-Publication entry:

Bufton, Melinda

Superette

ISBN   9781925780055

I. Title.

A821.3

Cover design by Miranda Douglas

This project has been assisted by the Australian Government through the Australia Council, its arts funding and advisory body.

Australian Government

Australia | Council
for the Arts

Contents

Heartstarter/New Project

After two weeks' rest you become
restless. Between dreams of kittens,
you meet the white horse in a field decorated for your moment.
What gives? you ask her.
She star jumps across your brow, leading you to
that secret *caffè* everyone has only whispered about. This is your payment.
After all of your tow-headed beliefs, the storm that breaks
gives you the new material you ordered. They'll make you sign for it, no exceptions.
You think Xanadu was made by set designers, and scant tinsel left from some
hack- tax write-off, buried before time?
It's not that simple.
Drive the mainstays to your farthest corner,
scissor in with the undertow. When the glues dries and the coffee sinks in:
a brand new shape.

Manufacture of the Pleasure Principle

Looking up feminist Ryan Gosling again
to use as a study aid you resist typing the words 'study aid' as
that gesture sublimes itself over.
All you see now is the competition memes,
which are not as textually useful. You are after the shortcut
to the male gaze. Back in the work world
you could cheat on this, preparing any page
of ideas and writing them off as 'roman à clef',
'strategy à clef'.

Ms Alterity

Frances Bean's twitter yields
Intricate value and maybe turns on a few
Popping bulbs in my mind, of late not too shiny.
She is in the photo looking like her mother, like Debbie Harry, also
weirdly like Madonna's daughter Lourdes
Wtf how does that even work, like some rock royalty family tree,
Always someone's cousin? at several thousand removes.
She has Darger as her wallpaper, and I have a neat book of poems
all about that ready in my reviewing in-tray.
Then, Mar 16, she tweets the cover of Definitely Maybe and says —
I swear —
'this album changed my life'
My favourite astrologer says Courtney displays a phoenix-like eminence
and I think again about how I can get
witchy.

Walking the Walk with My Sidelong L'Eggs

There is a Phaidon
coffee table splendour on
the history of *The Face*
coming out. I used to lust for Phaidon when
I wore a suit in the day and slipped greasy
into threads of phosphorescent night. I carried them
in a placco bag.

Tiger Musk Uppercut

Curl your lips round this
precipice of *grande* living. This acrid morning has
all the hallmarks of speed
shutter lens and emotional androgens.
Gold den. You are all so fresh. On point
these décor items speak a modern tongue; palms
are confident near block frame posters. I think this
is styled, though it did not exist in the video clip
Job Guide. When you bare your teeth
I am heat again,
fizzy in the artefact of compound
                        time.
Your custom-designed kimono with heavy smarts
backpocket fingerings
and knuckleback approvals.
                  'tabula rasa of your art rock hit'

Seamripper

You say to the tailor I'm looking for High Concept, and it makes for collaboration
so stretchy you don't even know when the elastic
will snap back. You know I used to work with this guy called Sam, and he told me
a story of a school friend. They were both boys, as it happened, in Manchester the
only
2 boys enrolled in Fashion for O levels. They corresponded. Let me tell you about
my friend, he invented a pair of pants SO LOW that the bum crack became a
beauteous cleavage. He was pleased but lamented
How will the lady wear her knickers? She won't, Sam laughed.
Mancunian tailors are all the rage, now.

> [Once she said she was saving
> for Manchester and our friend
> thought she meant
> SHEETS...]

You say to the tailor, I want the seams as flat as your two palms can
press them, easy on the steam eyes but apply your serger wherever a handstitch
cannot reach. Madam, this is difficult to say as customers never lie, but there is

> nowhere
> my handstitch
> cannot reach.

What silhouette is this

is this the shape of things to come?

Tangerine Crush

I mean, when are you gonna get over that dishevelled, cardigan wear
English teacher thing, like Professor Nada Surf as *crushée noblesse?*
Never. Never-say-ride-past-this-thing-moment.
Never say it can't be done.
The internodes are like slices of cartilage between your bones.
Those that were not meant to be cushioned. I am thinking
about bone a lot.
When a piece of music's good it starts with
a simultaneous burst in my throat, heart and nethers
and from there
is only a short ride to tears of super joy bursting from the lower corner
of my left eye. A sharpness of fidelity it's like when they invented television
and people would watch and stare and watch
through windows and watch. God. Would that
something could shock me like a television.

New Hair on the Streets

I have just seen the second example of what can only be called a

shag.

The other thing that they don't realise is that when they wear the large
glasses with a blonde bob
they look like their mothers.
Back when there were blouses and tweed skirts, back when menthol
over-rode your Charlie.
It's not bad. But it disrupts.
Not only does my brain register frump-acity
it messes with proper chronology.
Also, though, I just tried on high-waisted jeans that gave me a camel's hoof.
So round and smooth. if only you could go
rigid at the front and stretch over the arse.
Or whiskers that were really crunchy, concertinas so as to employ
front house style.

Conversations with Christopher Langton's
I luv you sculpture, 1993

'At the University of Melbourne'
You go to the Art Fair after a quick Office Hour of
Elizabeth Jolley, who is In Residence at U of M in that preppy
summer of your anxious hopes. You slip out a little short story for her to
look at. That's enough for you to feel cocksure and right.
Super unfolded,
You were wearing a tweed jacket and levis.
   Idol of the Real! A Clementine of men yet o so modern
   Wyatt Earp. Just in. With your
black Bonds t-shirts with soft-pack Marlboroughs tucked in the sleeve
don't think this went unnoticed
(undergraduate chicas, haha!)
In the corridors Miami Vice modernists swore ecru linen
    but that's another story.

'At the Art Fair'
This love device so canny
when unwound but fleeting in its
desperate lengths to stay inflated. I only live when I pump, it says
, so softly only I hear. It was a vending machine for my future patterns.
It makes grace like an external liver
cleanser. It will return you to silkier
plots,
disengaging character refs and all of your pert demands.
Mainly the tweed jackets were too boxy for
our legs. The proportions now make me
quiver, when I think how wrong. We had not dealt with the waists.

Girlfriend Experience

Nobody told me that *The Bell Jar* was funny
until the 50 year anniversary.
Can I have your memory bank of unperformed rites,
Just until tomorrow morning?? I'll bring it back
drycleaned.
On my open browser windows: buttermilk pancakes, *Rookie* magazine,
Sylvia Plath reads 'Daddy'
They're duskily small, my listening eyes, but
even with this squint I see her power reverb.
You jot down some villanelles before the clock-on, shouting YES YES
at your genius thought sprockets.
It serves you up from a dusty packet and all you have to do is wait for
the milk waterfall, all the way down your breezy swimsuit.
You laugh. You invoice.
Light a musk cigarette, contemplating
Spring.

Internship

Let the story go far enough to
profile-land. Let the subs allow you to watch
while they eat prawn cakes and smash deadlines to kingdom's
arse. What rain, what thunderstorm?
You have been given a delicate task, let
by-lines be morsels of hope, pet the worst kind of monster
in her silk-striped habitat as she
once knew the model for costings. But enough already
'another day, another project'. They are ciphers, and
that's their mossy piece. Hold history like glycerine holds water.
Can great skin be created?
You are the peach magnolia, it goes, and
future already hung out like a nylon knicker from a
twenty-third floor window.
Where is the future box? I'd like to cast my vote.
Fortune cookie, stumped again?
This field of enquiry is too short for my worldliness-cum-plans.

Stephanie, *Saturday Night Fever* — Assistant Editor, Virago

I fancy that later on
She went to London for a bit.
Somehow came across Carmen Callil at a party and perhaps
Read some ms's from the slush pile
On a piece work basis, casually.
It was cold there, but she is like the little match girl
poised near a 1920s gas heater
striking off the ms's one by one.
The pile grows larger with each cigarillo she smokes
her intent is largely literary.
But we knew that she was still finding a way to
display those things she found in Friedan and Greer.
Ultimately her accent gets in the way and she goes to
California where the air is more kind to the skin
and does one of two adventures there for the destiny —
A) shares a house with a guy's guy she knew back in the day who
makes the rent and gin slings with equal good (so, on balance worth
the histrionics —*quel* cliché!)
and B) took *The Women's Room* seriously, aka wearing of ponchos
on long walks down a moody beach
as though having pulled herself away from domestic slavery
as though she had been married but had somehow forgotten she really
skipped that step.

Gevinson

The advertising analysts have taken Tavi Gevinson and
Put her in a truth bath; they want to get to the bottom of her
Delight.
We're looking for the appeal, where it lives in her organism, looking to isolate it,
where it can
Be applied to. She is floating – it makes her think of being a comb in a barber shop
sterilising jar – the blue is a good light cerulean – and plotting her next silence.
Good for her. She will teach us all how to withhold.

It is the last thing left to be taught.

Endpeepers

Draft up your hell bent.
The stealing of a mailing list we call
untenable. You remember discovering by accident
the meaning of goodwill.
A quantity of ardour to be bought by the job-lot or
more specifically, as an adjunct to tape-measured assets.
A mailing list has many parts;
the reassurances spread with every cubic inch that
what we have say will be heard (or that what we must decry will
be dread). Your stenographer lifts her pencil to make marks or
would if she had more time. Animal instinct is
the search and replace and she is sure that she corrected
those salutations yesterday. Finishing School:
100% per cent full of girls with previous mark-up skills. There is no
more paper, people. We are fresh out. We are full of claims for the printed
Work and nothing in the (work) purse to show for it. There is no point bleeding
the sads for the way a double page spread would have
looked. The reality is nigh, and internship has
become a fancy price for a tardy skillset. Still. The mailing list will out.
This claiming of the hotspot
can only stretch our possibles to
the highest penetration. Uptake? About three for every listed, real name.

Hysterical Realism

Maybe if you put an elkhorn fern in the corner
maybe just stylistically if you did that,
bringing together the masterpiece of your daily aesthetic.
On the blog, it says to have too many of the good things in one
            place
Pinterest for the person you hope to become and not before
time.
It's all very recordable but not much in the bricks and mortar.
Choose a different colour way.
I cannot pose for the photographer until I have the right
thought, this way my design work will get its rightful singsong.
I have not done the media release myself,
really no cash for publicist.
Enhance all the blogistics I can with this little mac air
Sweep all the daily living things into some sort of large device
designed for hiding how we all catalogue our dirty starts.
So many unfinished projects, so much likelihood so little
chance of operating without an EFTPOS machine.
And what if you can't negotiate a tenancy within 3068?
I cannot go back
to being a lawyer
and I cannot find the Porter paint in Comeliest Eggshell.

Aunt Auntie

There is the devil and *l'ange*
That's angel to you
Concocting plans for the pathways
Knowing their freedom and hating it.
I am an auntie twice over, each little devil and angel for each little
One multiplied over my mantle shoulders.
There is also the non-familial, I am this for at least one little
Girl. We called her auntie but she wasn't, says the
Child, later in the century, when grown. To clarify, to gain.
To drop it down to the level it occupies.
Here are the jobs of Aunties:
To remove the scales of the gryphon, milk the cow, daily
Be good at fancywork, be quiet about longing,
Be all kinds of maiden, not the one of honour but nonetheless
Extremely *au fait* with honour. Strip the motorbikes' engine if necessary
Be plucky. Understand adventures, understand when to never tell
how good these are how these can be delicious like green undergrowth,
new milk, the purest liquor on the back of your throat
How these don't involve children. Like Nanny, from the Professor,
or Mary Poppins, you do the kind But responsible things
involving fresh air and wholesome fun with the little people
Later you can rest amongst whatever tangled art
and substance-fuelled harmpots you call those salons you host
In a kimono, from the war. You had a fiancé from that also, the war,
and then he was swallowed up
By this. 'I lived through WWII and all I got was this whore's kimono!'
So many aunties, then. So many devils angels.
Be proud and taciturn in equal parts. Choose not to be available.
Choose not to be other people's spare. As an Auntie I am my nephews'
second-favourite girl;
a badge-like honour, a keening role.

I taught my best friend's daughter to wink age one.

My work is done.

Now back to the cavalcades and working out what else there is to learn/teach.

Aunts read newspapers. They know things.

Toni Basil as Mary, with Heart of Gold

Buy you a monkey face biscuit, take me to the top floor
armagnac. We are but layers in this
semi-professional production of the Styles of
Millie-Whore Canty (Diaries 1-37) where you play
Travis and I take on the rich salubrious task of
transactions. Tickets and jam dainties.
I snorfle from toothglass and say to you
Hasn't it ever worried you that rock operas don't seem
to contain any rock?
We are on the window seat with breeze whipping our earlobes blue but
do not care.
What *do* they have, you say with eyes shifty to the door.
Slippery but I've got the edge of your capelet
snitched under my heel. You're going nowhere, Triple Threat.
I make you list the ingredients: the possible, the wherewithal, acrimony,
dye. Wipe that sugar off your fingers.
Later, we decide to hitch to
All Sinners Harbour House for some myotherapy and
a hot ankle bath.
You on one side of the wall
me on the other. Hellcat shampoo all over my scalp.

Harajuku Girl

A non-Japanese harajuku girl bearing the immense risk of instead looking
Mad
Something about her Western limbs that just makes it
Fancy dress.
She climbs the escalators I can see up her frilled skirts
Tulle upon frill upon chilled upper leg.
Her socks go only part way towards redemption
But this is what socks do
They are compromise
They are half
Where is she going now
I hope it's not to stand beneath the clocks with all the other subcultures.
That
Would be naff.
And jejune.

Damon Albarn's Eyes

What is it like to be a pair of pretty things, just balanced
like durable eggs there in the paradigm
of twenty-first century
Bohemia?
When we saw the northern lights we were amazed.
We stopped just being somethings that people valued because of our
pretty surfaces. And started, you know, to have something to believe in.
As eyes, people expect us not to have opinions, or to be,
you know, motivated by causes. There are a lot of shitty things going on
in this universe. And we are lucky to be in a position to do something
about it. I mean, otherwise what is fame for? We look to other famous eyes,
such as the Eyes of Horus. This way, we are on-tracked
to our events. I spent the afternoon dating these out.
I did a lot of incentivising in those days.

Guilty Pleasure (or, Where Are My Mittens?)

Given a chance, I will gravitate
toward the Big American novel,
set in Iowa by preference,
and sink into its plain-speaking ways because

you either leave the farm
or you don't.

The Possible Dream (*Buying Jeans Online*)

I don't know. Does Eileen Myles think this much
about her jeans?
Probably not.
Creating the perfect poetry jeans is not as hard
as you think.
It requires patience, skill,
habitat and armoury.
How to be Parisian seems to be really
How to be Patti Smith, with hair serum.
Step 1: Have small breasts.
But collarbones.
Step 2: Take a tonic out of your bar fridge
and replace all the Evian with spite. It's chilled, therefore.
Not bitter.
'She buys very expensive shoes but never polishes them.'
Cool. I'm in.

Festival Circuit

Historical dramedy autobiog is so hot right now.
It just pains me to think of all the careful, polite well thought-out
women conducting their research at this or that
library. They lean to perch elegantly at the festivals
in their Mesop drapery
and have accolades, in the way that others of us have
a coke/hopeful somethings. I want to be at the festivals too. Dirtier.
Dirty bird.

Alimentary Bloomsday

She was the knockabout brere and I was her tinder hire
She had the knockabout lair and I was her tinder rabbit.
You think these tears are glycerine
but they are hot, desperate chokes of my abandon.
My tears! My fight! My armistice! My love
holed up inside my mind.
When I didn't write, my muse like a grimy toy bunny
waited in a very dank, badly furnished cave. You think this is extreme?
You think these tears are glycerine?
'We stand on the shoulders of giants', tuxedo t-shirts
clinging as their forebears. Too tight.

New York Facial

You are click-bait in your
hunting jacket,
fire time in your bottle-ship.
See how pulling the string erects the mast, see how
lifting the curse takes longer than the hour.
Take your whittled pipe to Stringfellows for a night and see how
to get sticky like Fuzzy Felt.
Little clubs and hungover ravens.
whispered treatise on the dandy shore.
Two thousand likes in the humming station.
Watch what happens in the Paul Smith crazy socks,
matriculated into the kind of wild peach
we have no measure for, now that organic can mean something
with all thorns removed.
That is the classiest load
I have ever viewed. No so much a pleasure sandwich
as a baguette of juicy riposte. Oh stop it, you're
making me hungry.

Number 3

The aggregate is slow, at times the sleeping status, surprising

This too-dear friend
from behind his james franco sometimes face
I would call it european but I don't know what that is
I don't know what it means to force down the edgebanks
Can't know what it means to not nest but be in locations
that for me are settings from the spy novels that feed me
mortars or signs
The piecemeal or the anteroom, the next

we work on our manifesto on the balcony that drapes us over the street
and under entropy
We could be in between but I would see it with my
three-dimensional generational aspects
most probably
And he would see it with his quick-talking and his mindfield.
Tenacious.
Settlements and plans laid like a skin over
what came so long ago.
These are like guarantees.
This folks, trust. This takes place so that you will never need to
employ your own full-time philosopher.
To, you know, just do the hacking.

Scully

I had a Scully bob
Yeah yeah for real
I used to look like that, and them and those
I wore a cheongsam to my best friend's twenty-first that was
so exacting
I had to sew myself into it
in various places.
This is not the place for nostalgia.
But then, if not a poem..?
I had one of those
I used to wear those
I had that.

Showrunner

How now present brow.
What is it you deliver subscribe to my
MONTHLY
BOX
chockful of small samples,
ambling through the winter aspect.
Ungainly like
Bambi.
Which is to say, legs drip with sweat from
isolating this muscle group too long but my sweat tendrils
up like the collective view
of cartoon propaganda as limbic device.
I tear you a new roll of cinema tickets each time you
heart me. This says nothing about
the new engine I've designed.

Take it in the spirit

He massages my neck then goes home
fortunately brideshead revisited is on and I have a copy
of esquire
with daniel craig on the front.
Lucky

How is it that I could have missed
that daniel craig played
ted hughes?
Quick

Pussé

My cat becomes the gazelle of her destiny plan
tells me her real name, Arabella,
peeps to the light with the eye of a marksman or
the shrewdness of something like side business, patently not
anything to do with us.
She has other fish to fry.
I wish she were not so blanket-coated or that I were furrier,
That we may pull on thigh-high musketeer boots together and run
sure-footed beyond the alpha darts,
into that place where black forest does mean loaded with cherries
and the stories coalesce like your grin, backwards.

Methodology

I ordered a five-pound bag of mixed poetry scraps

to be delivered pronto. When they arrived there was too much green, but I sorted
the pieces out anyway and made a pretty nice top.

Dear Everybody

Dirty Blonde (the Ballad of C, She Who Goes)

Grey pearl is the
best halfway point to
ecsta-static
Like the way dirty hair
forgives
but also
provides the wave u dream
for, the texture of a
night-wave glamour,
in the particles of your
luminescent
textures.

Glamour den,
do not give way for gleam.
Placing grief pockets
further
down makes it harder
To feel the swallow.
Carmeline, of heady soul
discount
Would like you to know that
she
is available.
Here a clarion bell,
there ascendance.
You are so already on this
way.
You are so already there, to.

Signature Enclosed

The jubilance of
grind takes us
further into the
wellspring of what
it is that we have
in those side moments
I like your slipper E
I like your concentrate
Maybe it's cause it's
what I was born into
the fever
of jungle fever disco
times, light in the low
musk
in the heavy ding ding
Ding-a-ling.
It must be approximate
Spring, dub sequence high
the elevator is lined with
Pinkish marble. It's dark
it's only when we reach
Whatever'th floor that we
engage the spell.
The documentation. You
remove the layers as
the paillettes and glitter
are the regulatory code.
Needs must wants.

Glistener Mix

you may be unable to
Undertake this
glistening code
Underthing
I want the bombshell
in high relief
the paste jewels of
your determinate
Arcs, strapping
your sweet
sweat flicks
on my highbrow
Make me want
solitude for days
100 per cent quality
Pop me out
You need this too
This juice
My climb-high
My reach
My juice
strawberry grape
flow
scented marker from
my dance hand, donc.
Pull off the lid. Draw
Where?
 All. Over.

Honey Socket (sincerest alms)

Ginger crackle your
mind is a trap
Steel trap for its
creamy disco
portholes, look look
The apricot lid
Flicker statement
We are coming close now
Full set of eyes,
Girls looking you in the
subtext.
What are you
thinking now,
fulsome Ginger?
We are of like.
Breath irregular
Glitter flush now
making its way
through scalp
through head
In wink of a thousand eyes
Lids half lowered in
gorgeous calamity you know
Every one of us now on
the fleeting edge
edge me once
twice take me there
mystical gang of
here no now
yes

Résolue

In the end so many decades
before the
glomesh handbag
Like so many pages
discarded from
debunked textbook;
file.
With time came
resourcefulness a certain
je ne sais how.
KO knuckledusters but
good clean manicure.
Thus contents when spilled
1 x enamel lighter
23 ct gold plated trim
1 x electric vinyl cream
Lipstick, in Always Future
I will inherit exigencies
far beyond my will-respect
Keys to Mercedes
Keys to primal
consciousness
Keys to office
Keys to glass ceiling
Valve release for
intensity build-up
Touche Éclat
Gilt pockets
Like blisters in my darkened
musk

Sure sure, but no.

(after *'The Imitation Game'* ABC-commissioned documentary about Marina Abramovic and some young artists being mentored by her in a public art project, which aired in 2015)

There is a generation gap btw the older, most
esteemed performance artist
   and this shining tribe of collecteds. (those stitchy fillers, her lips
propped about your psyche)
She is so sure of her
Practice.
I want to love her whole blanched almond.
The kids just want to develop stuff on their little macs. This would be fine if
it were fine. But it's a really
visible, publicly privately funded art project, with collaboration and
doing-while-people-watch kind of deal.
One girl comports a mattress.
In another moment, it's 1979 in somewhere that looks like
Bacchus Marsh, the godforsaken thistle country with dry grass
and tank water. And artists. So many artists,
who just by witnessing each others' acts with
intensity, and later with Beaujolais, make it all come together.
What now the gritty pitch? A pitch is not doing. A pitch is
a carefully crafted statement that we have trained them from babes
to pop, in order to get validations of my feelz.
The exposure without time to craft hurts like the one person
who went to the country in the kombi but
actually, has never yet produced any art. Or not any that she is happy to stand by.
Later she would become something like an art teacher, or an arts manager or an
          insomniac.

Certificate of Authenticity

These are the leaving socks
grey as a pelt, cosy as a heartbreak.
They wind their way to the platform of incendiaries
the giving call undefined.
You are nineteenth century, with hounds
at your feet, draped on the tussock
the import of your chin-raised porcelain feel
but you've never worn a maker's mark.
It is high twilight you moved on
but instead, from the weepy nexus of well-received high art attics
the holy strumpeting cloudburst — an anthology of your wiles —
is best kept as a set that you manufacture on demand.
You now realise that the pastoral was not just re sheep.
Bed it down with your animal woes.
Then, after the scenery has been painted —
when lilac hills will provide for any dramatic eventuality,
providing there's grass and wildflowers
and recitations and that dreamy queen portrait, stage left —
You should lick it back better with tear-duct paintbrush.
Like the fox cat, you will surely now dig in
the boxed collectible
of your best-dressed andragogy.

Did you mean *iteration*?

The gmail interpolators *algorithm* my message to be about love poetry
They are wrong, all it is is
That I sent you a poem and said
Love in my signoff.
To put the two together, presumptuous much, huh!
Machines – like data amoeba – sit back on their clever heels and think they are all
smugly knowing about love.
They are not.
Even HAL, you do not get this even though you hung out with that guy for ages.
In Japan, they labour yet to create these feeling machines
Always careful of the uncanny valley
And it wasn't until I was ensconced in your circular screen that I realised
When the trance soundtrack kicked in and the small images spun like the
Talking rings
That I realised this was the technology you had developed
This was the sphere you had written
The code for; in the all-encompassing round
My mind took off in some various syntheses as I realised how conversant we are.
I could recognise you,
By the concept.

Gloss Pot

There is the way you can cover your lid with a thick gloss
It's like sump oil for the soul you have become
You want staying power through the party,
So you do as the page says and pack pigment like
Desperate wiles.
But wait.
Who's desperate?
When the metanarratives are proven to be false, I will acquiesce
My need to prove this desideratum is as fused as this black cherry styling
I am too determined in its features, and I sound like a sock-mouthed apologist
When I
Defend him.
Is he really that bad for me?
Really? like a bag full of salted caramel made good by its limit stretching
It can get you some good art, and in less sensible moments I think of the months
Of milking ahead, removing the slightly toxic bits like a particular gland
You know you need to work around
When you're a sushi chef with a difficult fish
Ah, to Japan. I didn't mean to go there.
Imagery-wise.
I suspect this is infinite in the way of a never-inked tattoo
Hatched in that thoughtful version of myself that has the rockabilly hot roller
 Hair
When I saw that line of swallows, a tragic reflex — first born 1987, September
Issue, *Dolly* —
Emerged itself.
The incredible crush the arbitrary targets
Your essence in the song of a long gone objective.

Gingerette

So line is drawn, a chalky dare
too inured by the new
commotion to examine the strand.
This is and these are times of great latitude.
Production values high.
We cannot monetise the swift loop thoughts
on that episodic tantra of must.
Some buttons want popping.
The cockwits fall away as I
make way for your wrap tight arms
Nimble is as nimble wants
Bright fever spot
Bright bright star; no, pretty thing constellation.
What's hard on the uptake, divine my hidden neurals'
grace
up the thigh towards a better feeling.
Each sip I create a twelve-score eat-me plan.
Elegy much, my beating popster? Take it as riven.
Before we start you need collaboration
quintessence has my quarterly sum now.
Above all, the intricate squeeze.
What doesn't spill you takes you longer.

Name as Destiny

International DJ
Anton
Antoine
Mark
Armand

Artist Type The First
Astrid
Oliver
Zach
Emmaline

Artist Type the Second
Stephen
Tracey
Trent
Mark
Callum

Born in the Seventies/Public Servant/Cousin
Matthew
Tracey
Trent
Mark
Anthony

Welfare worker, sunglasses pushed back on her head, squinting into the light
Trish

Musician
Dan

Bridesmaid
Valmay

First-born rockabilly child
Ruby
Scarlett

Occasional Names
Rufus
Rupert
Aphrodite
Genevieve
Guinevere
Lucida
Mud

Acknowledgements

I am grateful to the editors of the following journals, newspapers, and anthologies in which some of these poems first appeared: *The Age, Cordite Poetry Review, ETZ, Rabbit Poetry Journal, Contemporary Australian Feminist Poetry, Best Australian Poems 2013*, and *Dear Everybody.*

www.ingramcontent.com/pod-product-compliance
Lightning Source LLC
Chambersburg PA
CBHW031007090426
42737CB00008B/723